PRINTHOUSE BOOKS PRESENTS

Pulsations of a Heartbeat

A second chance at love

T. Moniz

VIP INK Publishing Group, Inc.

Atlanta, Georgia

Copyright © 2019

T. Moniz / PrintHouse Books

Editor: Chaundra Brownlee

ISBN: 978-1-7923-1472-3

Cover designed by SK7

LCCN: #2019952788

Published: 11/28/2019

www.PrintHouseBooks.com

VIP INK Publishing Group; Incorporated

All rights reserved. No parts of this book may be reproduced in any way, shape, or form or by any means without permission in writing from the publisher, or the author, except by a reviewer.

Kevin and Rich have both experienced heartbreak and disloyal partners in their most recent relationships. Although it may seem like they have it all, when it comes to relationships, Kevin and Rich can't seem to catch a break. In the last two novels we got to see Kevin fall in love with Brittany and Rich tie the knot with Melissa, only to find betrayal after searching for love and commitment.

In this third series of Pulsations of a Heartbeat we get to see the story continue from Brittany's perspective. Brittany is a former exotic dancer who had big dreams of finishing school and owning her own spa one day.

While dating Kevin, he put her in a position to leave the strip club, and finish school so she could have exactly what she wanted. Now single and reaching success with her new spa called The Sanctuary, change is coming Brittany's way whether she's ready or not.

As her life transitions into this new journey she can't help but feel like something's missing. It has always been easy to get a man with money, but it's hard to find someone who really loves you for you. Will Brittany take a second chance at love? Or will her old player habits die hard?

T. Moniz
PULSATIONS OF A HEARTBEAT III

www.PrintHouseBooks.com

Table of Contents

Brittany and Melissa……………..7

Single Again……………...………….28

The Sanctuary………….....……….46

A second chance at love……..71

Drew…………….……….....………..86

Unexpected Guests……………..100

Fool me once shame on you..133

Fool me twice shame on me…152

1. Brittany and Melissa

Needles shot through Brittany's petite firm body as she looked up and saw Kevin and Rich watching her stroke Melissa with her 10-inch strap on. Melissa moaned face down into Rich's bed, begging Brittany not to stop as they were caught in the act. Pleasure, anger, and disappointment filled the room with so much tension, it began hard for everyone to breathe properly. Brittany, startled by Kevin's presence jumped up, snatched off her strap on, and frantically threw her dress over her head.

Rich:

So fucking ya boss wasn't enough, you go after my best friend's triflin' ex?

Brittany:

Triflin?!

Melissa:

Rich let me explain I know this looks bad I just came to get my clothes and...

Rich:

And what she slipped and fell on you with a strap on?!

Kevin didn't say a word. Shocked and disappointed he removed himself from the dramatics. Brittany ran after him not knowing

what she could say after being
caught in her ex's best friend's bed
with his just finalized ex-wife.

Brittany:

Kevin! Please...

Kevin:

Don't touch me Sapphire

Brittany:

Really Kev? Since when am I
Sapphire to you?

Kevin:

Since I don't know who you are,
and I guess I never did.

Brittany:

Kevin that's not true, can you please stop walking away, and turn around and talk to me!

Kevin:

AND SAY WHAT? You're sorry?

Brittany:

Look Kevin, I tried for you, I did but I'm single now, just like you. I heard about you bringing Sybil to the wedding after we broke up. I'm sure you weren't considering how I felt when you pulled that shit were you?

Kevin:

Look, she may have been trying to fuck me when we were together, but I never cheated on you Brittany. Not once! I was loyal to you, I gave you everything! Damn near gave you my last breath, and what did you give me hmm? I'll wait Sapphire. Tell me one thing you ever did to show you considered me?

Brittany:

Kevin.

Kevin:

WHAT.

Brittany:

I...

Kevin:

WHAT! EXACTLY. We both know your selfish ass can only be loyal to the game. J-Rock told me to be careful, and I should have listened.

Brittany:

J-Rock? How can you stand here and act like I didn't love you Kevin? I did everything you asked me to do. Not just for me but for us, so we could grow together. I was wrong for not coming to you first, but things were changing. I saw a pattern I've seen before. In my eyes it was smarter to move on, before I got played. So I started taking numbers and going on dates... I made a mistake.

Kevin:

You may be in a better position from when we met, but your mentality will always be the same. And by the time you're ready to change ain't no man going to be available for ya triflin' ass. All you care about is what somebody can do for you.

Kevin got in his car and drove off leaving Brittany standing there with nothing but his last words to sink in. There was no doubt about how much Kevin helped Brittany accomplish her dreams quicker. Kevin loved Brittany and helped her because he simply wanted to see her win. Brittany got in her brand new silver Mercedes Benz and started reflecting on how she met J-Rock.

It was J-Rock that convinced her to come by Club Ebony and make some real money. Brittany transitioned from bartending to stripping, which exposed her to a side of men nobody else would understand until you lived it for yourself. The regulars, the dope boys, the married businessmen, and the sugar daddies of course. Dancing was a small part to a bigger lifestyle of finesse and hustle. Like any beginner coming into this, she observed and watched how the other women made their money.

Blue took Brittany under her wing and taught her all the tricks she needed to know to make the most money every night. As Brittany drove home, she had a flashback of talking to Blue the first night she started dancing, while stopping at a red light. Blue's weave was 24 inches long, dyed bright blue, and perfectly parted down the middle. She had on a silver metallic thong that revealed her perfectly round peach shaped booty and a white transparent bandeau top that showed off her nipple piercings.

Blue:

Don't ever smile while dancing, you look more seductive when you keep a straight face. Always practice in the mirror, you should always have a couple signature moves that makes these niggas want to empty everything in their pocket. Get comfortable with the pole; niggas love the pole. The dope boys are generous. They understand our hustle so they always show love. If you don't know all your designers, and most expensive watches, learn them. You can come up on a long-term sugar daddy if you know what they're wearing. Sugar daddies usually have on the expensive suits; they love paying our bills just for our time.

Most of your money can be for play if you play your cards right with your clientele. The only thing that isn't worth your time is fucking for money, unless you really about that life then you want to make sure you stay in VIP. That's the only place there's a price tag on ya pussy.

You see Brittany, our body is their fantasy. If you understand the art, you'll understand how to always get what you need from them. You just have to learn the game, how you make your money every night is all on you. Take a shot, loosen up, and go make this money bitch.

The light turned green and Brittany's memories came to an end as she drove toward her new luxury apartment in the sky. Brittany finally had everything she always wanted. Business was going great at her new spa and now she was finally in Buckhead, her location of choice, living out her dreams.

She pulled into her new place and drove down to the parking garage and pulled into parking spot 23. Sluggish and drained from the drama that just took place, Brittany nonchalantly walked to the elevator. She swiped her key fob across the sensor and hit the 19th floor. The silver elevator doors opened and Brittany turned right and walked down to the corner unit at the end of the hallway. She unlocked her door, walked inside, and dropped her keys on her black granite surface island counter.

Coco, her teacup Yorkie, started hyperactively jumping around in her kennel. She let Coco out of her kennel and walked to the balcony where she had artificial turf laid across the cement, with a dog friendly play zone on the left and to the right were some lounge chairs where she liked to sit down and smoke a blunt before bed.

The skyline view of Atlanta glistened under the sunset shining directly through her crystal clear glass windows that surrounded her high rise luxury apartment. Brittany rolled a blunt and sat on her balcony watching the sunset go down with Coco thinking of Kevin and everything that led to this moment.

The next morning Brittany woke up with Coco on her chest on her white leather couch in her living room. She got up and walked into her master bedroom. Brittany picked up her iPhone and gave Melissa a call to make sure she was okay after Rich and Kevin caught the two of them in his bed.

Melissa:

Hey Brit.

Brittany:

Bitch are you okay? I'm sorry I left you hanging, but when I saw Kevin standing there I damn near pissed on myself!

Melissa:

Girl after walking onto the balcony and finding all my stuff burned up, I was so upset. You were there for me; one thing may have led to another but it's not like we planned to have sex in Rich's condo.

Brittany:

Girl the look on their faces was priceless. I mean I was surprised, but I couldn't tell if they were pissed off or turned on! Ha-ha

Melissa:

I don't know about Kevin, but once you two walked out Rich was definitely turned on.

Brittany:

Why, what happened?

Melissa:

Last night took a turn I never saw coming, it was crazy. We stood there arguing for minutes, and the whole time I had forgot I was standing in front of him naked. I started to notice his eyes wandering, and his tone of voice got lower and lower. We went from arguing to having sex within minutes.

Brittany:

Wait what? You and Rich?

Melissa:

Maybe the whole situation kind of turned him on? Once he apologized about my clothes, I started to apologize about William, one thing led to another and we just lost control.

Brittany:

If pussy isn't power, I don't know what is. I thought I had skills, but I would have never been able to pull that shit off with Kevin!

Melissa:

Cut it out, I feel bad about what happened. We may not be together anymore, but I think we needed that moment. Rich may not have been perfect, but he was good to me. I never meant to step out on our marriage; it was just bad timing.

Brittany:

You think y'all are going to work it out?

Melissa:

Our divorce is final now, so I don't think so. I love Rich, but we both know that's a commitment I can't handle right now. I'm ready to be single, and answer to no one. After last night I think he gets it.

Brittany:

You think so? Even after the sex?

Melissa:

Rich started seeing Joyce ,she's been a cashier at his shop for years. She was there for him when he found out about William, and now he's moving her into his condo. Which is why they walked in on us, because they were moving her stuff in.

Brittany:

Shut the fuck up, are you serious? See that's exactly why I never liked Kevin doing business with Sybil. Niggas love mixing business with pleasure.

Melissa: It gets crazier.

Brittany: How crazy?

Melissa: She walked in on us having sex.

Brittany: No she didn't bitch!

Melissa:

She did, and she wasn't upset at all, she joined in, and I'm actually just now heading home.

Brittany:

I always knew your fine ass was a freak.

Melissa:

I'm single, and it feels good to finally own it. By the way, can you fit me in at the end of the week in the Oasis room? After this, and the week I have ahead I'm in need of a spa day.

Brittany:

Absolutely, I need all the details about your love triangle anyway! My last client's at 2 on Sunday, come by around 4. I'll reserve the Oasis room for the rest of the evening.

Melissa:

That sounds amazing, I'll see you soon.

    Brittany smirked at the unexplainable series of

unfortunate events she and Melissa had. It was Kevin and Rich's friendship that brought Brittany and Melissa together. Luckily they remained friends after both relationships didn't end up working out. Brittany hopped out of bed and went through her closet to find something sexy to wear to work. She brushed through her designer clothes and stopped on the navy blue Armani suit Kevin bought her for her interview as an executive assistant for Selena.

She reminisced about the day he made the call and surprised her with this outfit to start her new life. It was Kevin's recommendation that got her out of the strip club and working better hours to finish school.

Kevin's last words replayed in Brittany's head as she tried to shake off her emotions and convince herself she didn't miss Kevin. Brittany grabbed her brand new black Prada dress and matching shoes, got dressed and headed to The Sanctuary.

2. Single Again

Kevin left work early Monday afternoon. He pulled into his 3-bedroom 4-bathroom, single level abode on West Paces Ferry Road. After pulling into his 6-car garage Kevin strolled inside and immediately threw off his shoes on to his dark bamboo floors, while he removed his blazer. He grabbed his shoes and went straight into his walk-in closet to change into his work out attire.

He changed into a navy blue, sleeveless, workout shirt and a pair of matching blue Adidas basketball shorts. Kevin grabbed an old pair of grey retro 11's and threw his gym bag over his shoulder. He grabbed the keys to his black Maserati and headed straight to the courts to relieve some stress.

After he played a couple games, he stopped by Rich's shop to get his car detailed and waxed.

Kevin:

What's going on Rich?

Rich:

Kev, what's up bro. It's Monday, you not working late tonight?

Kevin:

Nah I left work early, I just haven't been able to focus lately, so I decided to go hoop and relieve some stress.

Rich:

Why don't you call Sybil and relieve stress the right way?

Kevin:

She's pullin' up later. She's been texting me all day. I almost feel like she's using me for sex.

Rich: What's wrong with that?

Kevin:

Nothing, these women are just different now, it scares me. She's so aggressive.

Rich:

Sometimes you got to accept people for who they want to be. I had a crazy night with Joyce and Melissa.

Kevin: WHAT?

Rich:

I know, I still can't believe it myself.

Kevin:

How the hell? After we caught her with Brittany?

Rich:

(tsk) I was screaming at her, and she was just standing there butt naked, trying to defend herself. I'm a man, I couldn't help it, she was looking good. Next thing I know she face down in my pillows and Joyce walked in.

Kevin:

Y'all have a serious problem with not locking doors.

Rich:

Man, she stood there watching us, and as soon as I noticed she was there, she walked in and joined. No explanation, no exchange of words, nothing. I think want to marry her.

Kevin:

Woah, that's the last thing you should be thinking about! Where does this leave you and Melissa?

Rich:

We cool; We talked it out, and hey I get it, she wasn't ready for commitment. I don't see why we can't stay friends now.

Kevin:

You just want a guaranteed threesome at all times.

Rich: Damn right I do.

Kevin:

So just like that, a threesome takes all the pain away?

Rich:

I'm not saying that, but I can't stay mad forever. She's human; she did me wrong, and because we have some sort of love for each other, we found a way to move forward. I'm happy with Joyce, but Melissa was once someone I wanted to spend the rest of my life with. That don't go away overnight, this could be our way of a second chance. Might as well make peace with a love language that works for us.

Kevin:

Can't argue with that. Look Rich, if you like it, I love it. Just be careful.

Rich: Where's the fun in that?

Once Kevin's car was waxed and detailed, he went straight home to shower and get comfortable for his evening with Sybil. They had been texting each other all day, and he was expecting her to arrive at any minute.

Kevin walked into his kitchen and grabbed a bottle of wine from his wine cellar area and popped open the cork of his favorite Pinot Noir. He prepared a medium rare steak with his special homemade mashed potatoes. Kevin appreciated sharing a good meal with a beautiful woman, and it also helped him keep his mind off of Brittany.

Kevin always thought Sybil was an attractive woman, but he

always held his composure out of respect for Brittany. After they broke up Kevin stopped fighting what was being thrown at him, and simply started to enjoy himself. She had been over a couple times since Rich and Melissa's wedding, but Kevin made an effort not to make it a habit, since Sybil was still technically one of his clients.

    Fortunately, he knew Sybil was only one call away when he needed a stress reliever like tonight. As he walked down the hallway, he stepped on an unexpected dog toy. Brittany's dog Coco was always stashing her toys in random spots. Kevin almost smirked at the thought of Brittany's dog running around the house, while they would be laid up around the house together. As he stared at the toy the doorbell rang. Sybil was right on time.

He threw the toy in the trash, opened the door and couldn't believe what he found. Sybil stood there in a silky high black ponytail wearing a long trench coat, with black patent leather Christian Louboutin heels on.

Sybil: You ready for dinner?

Kevin: What's on your menu?

Sybil: Me.

Kevin moved aside to let her enter. She walked in like she was walking on a runway. She stopped and faced Kevin to unwrap her beige ankle long trench coat, and let it drop to the ground. Her smooth cocoa skin complimented her curves, allowing her full D cup breasts to sit on her chest patiently waiting to be caressed. Kevin stood there and watched her while she walked toward him. He grabbed her by the waist as she leaned in and wrapped her arms around his neck. She kissed him softly, and he lifted her up in the air and pulled her legs in to wrap around his waist.

Kevin led her into his bedroom where he devoured everything on Sybil's dinner menu. He turned over and fell straight to sleep while Sybil made herself at home. She sat in the kitchen in one of Kevin's t-shirts, drinking a glass of Pinot Noir and nibbling at the steak they never ended up eating on Kevin's dinner menu.

Sybil sat there with a smirk on her face completely satisfied of how her evening ended.

Kevin was enjoying his time with Sybil, but he knew it was strictly physical attraction. He was enjoying the sex but his heart wasn't in it. He always found a reason to get up early the next morning, so Sybil wouldn't get too comfortable. They talked everyday through text but mostly because Sybil held most of the conversation. Kevin was hesitant to take anyone serious after Brittany. The cynical side of him wanted to push the thought of real love existing to the side, so he can focus on getting money. Of course, the other side of Kevin wanted to give love a second chance.

A few days after Sybil's visit to Kevin's house, it suddenly became difficult trying to hold a conversation with Kevin. He wasn't responding much to any of Sybil's text messages and when he did, he told her he was busy. Sybil being the type of woman who normally wouldn't get ignored, decided to pop into Kevin's office and say hi.

Sybil:

Good afternoon I hope you're not busy, I was in the area and thought I'd stop by.

Kevin:

Not a problem Sybil, I was just about to shoot you an email with an update on your Atlanta property.

Sybil:

Sounds great. You know Kevin I can't thank you enough, you have been so good to me since the first day we met.

Kevin:

I'll always make sure you're in good hands.

Sybil: Am I?

Sybil placed her Louis Vuitton purse on Kevin's desk and started unbuttoning her satin cream blouse. Kevin gave her an intense tired gaze as she glided behind his mahogany coated desk and pulled his chair out. Sybil smirked as she pulled her pencil skirt up and bent down to unbutton Kevin's freshly steamed black dress pants.

Kevin:

Sybil, I'm working, right now's not a good ti... oooooh.

    Sybil stroked the top of Kevin's hard large imprint poking out of his dress pants, revealing what he really wanted. Staring directly in his eyes while he fell into temptation, she pulled out his penis and started to French kiss it softly. She looked up at Kevin and began to stroke him with a firm grip while watching him grow weak.

Sybil:

I knew when Brittany told me about you, she didn't deserve you. I always get what I want.

As Sybil reached up for a kiss Kevin stopped and turned his face after the striking comment she just made.

Kevin: What'd you just say?

Sybil: She didn't deserve you baby.

Kevin:

Is that why you told her we were sleeping together before it was actually true?

Sybil:

(giggles) I was only joking with her, but the look on her face was priceless. I was waiting for her to bring it up again to tell her it was a joke, but she never did. She started dating Drew instead.

Kevin: Huh? Is that really funny to you?

Sybil:

Baby relax, it all worked out perfect now we can be together.

Kevin stopped and leaned back in deep thought and then started buckling his pants back up.

Sybil:

What. What's wrong?

Kevin:

I always thought a woman who has to lie and be deceitful was unattractive. And honestly, I'm completely turned off, so with all due respect Sybil, I have to get back to work.

Sybil:

I was just trying to help you see the type of woman you deserve, but if you can't see all of this in front of you, then you're not the man I thought you were anyway.

Selena knocked on Kevin's office door twice and walked in after hearing no response.

Selena:

Oh, I'm sorry, I didn't know you were seeing someone at the moment.

Kevin:

It's ok Selena, Sybil was just leaving.

Sybil snatched her purse off of Kevin's desk and walked off with an attitude. Giving Selena the stare of death as she walked by her fixing the buttons to her blouse as she made her exit.

Selena:

Everything alright Kevin?

Kevin:

Everything's fine, I'm just tired of giving my time to those who don't deserve it.

Sybil:

Amen. I'm not trying to get in your business Kev, but if you ever want to talk, my door's always open.

Kevin: Thank you Selena, but I'll be fine.

3. The Sanctuary

After a long week Brittany sat in her neatly kept modern style office eating lunch at her clear acrylic desk before her last client came in at 2 pm. Her receptionist Natalie wore a dark and soft pixy cut that resembled Halle Barry with a beautiful yellow sundress to compliment her smooth chocolate skin with her tall slim frame.

She was a natural young beauty with a pearly white smile that made anyone effortlessly smile back. She walked into Brittany's office with a bouquet of red roses in a beautiful red vase. Natalie gently sat the roses down on Brittany's desk beside her laptop.

Natalie:

I want to be just like you when I grow up Boss Lady

Brittany:

Roses. Again?

Natalie:

That's the third bouquet of roses you got this week, and they all say XOXO Drew. Your vagina must be gold girl.

Brittany:

You crazy, he's just an old friend.

Natalie:

Well can you lend me one of those old friends, cause my man won't even take the trash out for me, and you got men and women doing whatever you want...

Brittany:

Girl please that's just how it looks, that's far from the truth.

Natalie: So, you like Drew?

Brittany:

He used to be one of my regulars at Ebony. He knew me when I started bartending, and he saw me transition into dancing. He always wanted us to be something more, but I didn't want to make things complicated with work. A couple months ago I left The Sanctuary and stopped by Ebony to go show my ladies some love, pass out some business cards, and have a drink. Drew was there and now that he knows I'm no longer dancing he keeps shooting his shot, but I don't know.

Natalie:

Sounds like he's always loved you.

Brittany:

It's possible, or he just wants what he can't have.

Natalie:

So, you don't want to be with him?

Brittany:

It's not that... it's just complicated.

Natalie:

You still love Kevin, don't you?

Brittany:

Natalie, are you going to ask me 21 questions about my love life, or are you going to be the great receptionist I love, and make sure my next client is waiting out there for a beautiful young lady to greet them?

Natalie:

See how smooth that was, that's how you got roses 3 times this week.

Brittany:

Are you done Natalie?

Natalie:

Your last client is Selena, she'll be getting a facial and a wax.

Brittany:

Oh perfect, she'll be here right at 2, she's never late.

Natalie:

I'll bring her to your station, but listen boss lady, whenever you're tired of being a player, just pass me the ball cause I'm wide open.

Brittany laughed, and rolled her eyes as her crazy receptionist walked out of her office. She grabbed the note attached to the roses and smirked. She headed over to greet Selena who walked in at 2 pm on the dot. Selena's coffee brown eyes lit up and her skin was already glowing from her fresh blow out.

Brittany:

Hi, Selena! It's so nice to see you. Oh my gosh look at your hair, you look beautiful.

Selena:

Thanks Brittany, it's so nice to see you! I love this place; it really is becoming my favorite spa, I've been telling all my clients about it.

Brittany:

I appreciate you so much, you know I'll throw all of y'all in the Oasis room just let me know, don't hesitate.

Selena:

If you know me at all, you know I won't ha-ha.

Brittany:

Let's get you started I have this amazing new mask; it's supposed to smooth out and take all the dead skin off leaving an even bright tone.

Selena:

Mm let's do it.

Brittany:

How's business?

Selena:

Business is great, but I have to admit things have been a bit off in the office lately. I know you and Kevin aren't together anymore, but maybe you should reach out and see how he's doing

Brittany:

(Sigh) I don't know Selena. I can't lie, I do miss Kevin, but things are complicated right now. He kind of walked in on me and Melissa... in Rich's bed last week.

Selena: Wait...

Brittany:

I know girl I know, it's as crazy as it sounds. I just couldn't help myself! After it happened, Kev and I exchange words, I brought up the whole Sybil situation, and he still made sure I knew everything was all my fault...

Selena: Wait Sybil? Sybil Cannon?

Brittany:

Yeah, I'm sure you know her, she's one of Kevin's clients.

Selena:

She's actually the client that Kevin just let go, and from the looks of it he had a good reason.

Brittany: Girl spill the tea

Selena:

(sigh) I walked in on her buttoning up her blouse, she looked upset. I tried to leave but he insisted I stay because she was leaving. It seemed like she came on to him, and he turned her down.

She walked out and gave me the meanest stare a girl could give. She would have got slapped if I wasn't in a brand new Dolce & Gabbana blouse.

Brittany:

She was my mentor from school. She took me under her wing and gave me all the resources and I needed to get my spa together. Next thing I know she's doing business with Kevin and having lunch dates with him. Never once mentioned to me she went to see him at his office. After Kevin informed me, she was constantly coming on to him and being inappropriate, I finally said something. She went on to tell me that her and Kevin had slept with each other on several occasions. I should have gone to Kevin but I don't know, I guess I just believed her.

I convinced myself he'd rather be with a woman like Sybil, so I stopped answering his calls, and decided to move on. She mind-fucked me, but it was my fault because I didn't communicate with Kevin, and I should have. I started seeing someone else, and he caught him coming out of my apartment. He was so pissed, he threw my phone against the wall and made sure I knew that I fucked up our relationship. To put the icing on the cake now he thinks I'm fuckin' with Melissa.

Selena:

Well this explains a lot, Kevin hasn't been acting like himself, maybe he misses you too. Try reaching out to him, I know he's hurt, but everything you two went through only sounds like miscommunication, not because you didn't love each other.

Brittany:

Idk Selena, things are different now, so much has changed in such a short time frame.

Selena:

Well it doesn't hurt to say hello and how are you doing.

Brittany:

Enough about me, where you going and why do you look so fine today?

Selena:

On a date! I've been seeing this guy, he's not what I'd normally go for, but change is good right?

Brittany: Right...

Selena:

Sometimes we have to take chance with what we're not used to, and just do what feels right.

Everything Selena was saying resonated with how Brittany felt about herself. Brittany sat there thinking about Kevin as she finished up Selena's wax. Melissa arrived just as Selena finished up and was heading out the door.

Melissa:

Knock-knock, did I show up too early?

Brittany:

Hey Melissa! No not at all, we were just finishing up. Melissa this is Selena, I worked for her before I opened my spa.

Selena:

So nice to meet you, I've heard great things about you.

Melissa: Likewise.

Selena:

Thank you so much Brittany for squeezing me in last minute, I'm going to head out so I can arrive on time.

Brittany:

Have fun boo, don't do anything I wouldn't do on the first date.

Melissa:

So, you can pretty much do anything in that case.

Brittany:

Melissa!

Melissa:

I'm only joking

Melissa smirked at Brittany as Selena headed out to dinner. The two of them changed into some fluffy white robes and relaxed in the Oasis room. The Oasis room was a reservation only room for members only. It was the Oasis room that made her membership plans at The Sanctuary really popular. It was set up like an indoor Oasis experience.

There was a small rock textured waterfall that created a flowing stream around the waterhole like swimming pool. It was a saltwater pool that shimmered a crystal blue color. The hot tub had fresh rose petals floating in the water. The lighting in the room was lit low and intimate. The aroma of fresh mint leaves and scented oils filled the room with a calm sensation.

The floor was covered with artificial turf and palm trees dispersed in each corner of the room. Brittany had two massage therapists that gave you a full body oil massage. She had unlimited champagne, with full body exfoliating treatments, and product sample gift bags. No more than two separate reservations at a time were allowed in this room for parties no bigger than 10. The Oasis room became so popular her members started buying it out for bachelorette parties and small events.

Beauty was accepted at all times in the Oasis room so the option to be fully robed or nude was to each member's discretion. J-Rock often bought out this room to treat the girls at Club Ebony.

Needless to say business was great at The Sanctuary. It was slowly becoming an Atlanta hot spot for every woman.

They spent the evening discussing their spontaneous night gone wrong. The two of them drank champagne and relaxed after getting a full body massage and finishing where they left off, before they were interrupted in the condo. Brittany and Melissa were enjoying this new chapter of their friendship, they had fun together without attaching personal emotions into their sexual attraction for each other.

The two of them continued the rest of the night at Brittany's place where they discussed business, love, and great sex all night over wine and new face mask samples. They began to discover that sex can always be on the table with their friendship, as long as they keep honesty in the core of it all.

Brittany sat in her office Monday morning scrolling through her computer doing research on ingredients. She was looking into making her own skin care product. She opened up a file of saved pictures in her laptop to add more to her vision board. As she went through her saved photos, she stumbled on a picture of her, Kevin, Melissa, and Rich all hanging out in Kevin's backyard.

She sat there thinking about her conversation with

Selena. Adrenaline hit Brittany hard and pulsations of her heartbeat began to speed up. Upon impulse Brittany picked up her phone to call Kevin. "If he doesn't pick up by the fourth ring just hang up!" She calmly said to herself as she pressed call. Brittany sat there with a new breath of anxiety at the thought of rejection as the phone rang a second time.

After the second ring she put her phone down on her desk and placed it on speaker phone with her finger next to the end button to get ready to hang up, and say it was an accident. Once it hit three regret was overflowing her mind and then she heard his voice.

Kevin:

Hello...

Brittany:

Kevin, hey I was sitting in my office and I think I was... I'm looking for... well I'm making my own skin care product, but do you want to sit down and talk over dinner maybe?

Kevin:

... okay, um what's your schedule like on Sunday?

Brittany:

Sunday is perfect my last client's at 1:30 pm I should be home and ready by 6

Kevin:

Okay, I can do 6.

Brittany:

Okay perfect I'll see you Sunday.

Brittany hung up wearing a smile. She started to like the idea of her and Kevin hanging out again.

    Kevin sat at his office desk staring at his phone after hanging up with Brittany. He couldn't figure out what made him pick up the phone, but he cracked a smile at her sudden effort to see him. Kevin loved Brittany even though she hurt him once, he couldn't help but hope she learned a lesson from these experiences.

    He watched her change while they were together once before, and he couldn't help but wonder was she ready to fully commit this time. Kevin's vivid daydreams of him and Brittany suddenly dissolved by an incoming text from Sybil.

Sybil:

Dinner reservations for 7:30 at Ruth Chris

Kevin:

???

Sybil:

I shouldn't have bothered you at work baby, we can start fresh tonight over dinner.

Kevin:

Tonight, won't work for me. Sybil, I don't think we should see each other anymore.

Sybil:

You're just stressed; I'll come by tomorrow and give you a massage.

Kevin, confused and annoyed with Sybil's persistence, put his phone down and got back to work. He knew ignoring a beautiful woman like Sybil wasn't going to be easy, but the way she was acting was a huge turn off. Kevin knew he never saw a real future between him and Sybil anyway.

He enjoyed her conversation and the sex was good, but there was something about her that made it hard for him to take her seriously, and their circumstances of how they met played a big part. Kevin always felt like Sybil's intentions from the start never came from a genuine place. For those reasons he intuitively kept his distance.

4. A Second Chance at Love

Brittany arrived a few minutes after 6 at Poor Calvin's. Kevin was already seated waiting for her. She glided through the restaurant in a beautiful satin black dress with her hair pulled back into a sleek ponytail that went straight down her back. Her favorite Versace scent that was also Kevin's favorite traveled through the restaurant as she floated by, creating an elegant aroma to match her soft appearance.

Kevin looked up from the table and was speechless. It was like the first time he saw her at Club Ebony. He stood up at the sight of her beautiful presence, gave her a hug and pulled out her chair.

Kevin:

You look beautiful Brit

Brittany:

Thank you

They both stared at each other holding back a smile. Their love and attraction for one another was still present, and extremely hard to hide. Kevin wasted no time ordering a round of drinks for the two of them. There was still a nervous tension between them even though how they felt for each other was obvious. The best way to break the ice was over a few shots of Don Julio.

Kevin:

I haven't been here in a while; I'm actually excited for this lobster fried rice.

Brittany:

The food is so good here, I've been craving some fried green tomatoes since last week.

Kevin:

We got to order a few of those, you know I love tomatoes.

Brittany:

Bet, we'll get two orders of fried green tomatoes and dessert for later.

A petite brown waitress came over with her braids pulled up into a crown like bun in all black and smile that resembled Gabrielle Union with deep dimples. They ordered some appetizers and two double shots of Don Julio. Once they took a shot together, they wasted no time letting the tequila kick in and do the talking. It was time to stop avoiding the elephant in the room and have a discussion.

Brittany:

Look Kev, I'm sorry about everything. I never meant for you to find us like that. I was always attracted to her, and the more time we spent together, I just... Melissa and I are just friends.

Kevin:

It was weird I can't even lie; I didn't even know you liked girls. I'm not judging you, but it just made me realize how much I didn't know about you. I was so focused on seeing you level up for your future; I didn't take the time to get to know you for you in the present moment.

Brittany:

I should have never listened to Sybil. I should have come to you, but I'm so used to men cheating, and women coming with the facts, all I wanted to do was remove myself, and try to forget about you. I never meant to ruin what we had. I just assumed she was the better woman for you, and with all the time you spent with her, I convinced myself you liked her.

Kevin:

Brittany, I never wanted Sybil. There's no doubt that she is a successful, attractive woman, but I already had my trophy. I did the right thing, and I could have cheated on several occasions, but I didn't.

After I found out you were seeing somebody else, out of frustration and spite I started seeing Sybil. It wasn't until she made a comment about sabotaging our relationship, that made me cut her off. I don't think any woman should take pride in lying and ruining relationships to get what they want. I could never trust a woman like that.

Brittany:

I'm sorry Kev, I know you think my mentality will never change, but it has and I'm still learning how to become a better me every day.

Kevin:

I know that's true because I never expected you to call.

Brittany:

You can thank Selena for that. She was at The Sanctuary not too long ago, and said she was worried about you. She also mentioned you dropped Sybil as a client.

Kevin:

I did. She was doing too much.

Brittany:

Well Kev, I know things aren't going to happen overnight, but I'd love for us to spend more time together, I do miss you.

Kevin:

I miss you too Brittany, and I'm very proud of everything you're doing with The Sanctuary.

Brittany:

Thanks Kevin, I really appreciate that.

Kevin:

I always knew you'd be great.

Brittany:

Why don't we get dessert to go and finish talking at my place? I live in Buckhead now.

Kevin:

Oh, you fancy huh? All that money must be coming in quick, you got the Mercedes and you Buckhead livin' now?

Brittany:

Whatever Kevin, is that a yes?

Kevin:

It depends on what dessert you're trying to get.

Brittany:

I am the dessert.

Kevin:

I'll get the check.

Kevin and Brittany were back at it like they never left, and things were going great. Sundays went back to being their quality time days, and business was better than ever for the both of them. The closet space she once had at Kevin's house began to fill back up, and he even got a space for himself in her closet.

Things felt better this time around for Brittany, because this time she felt more like an equal financially. She didn't need Kevin, she wanted Kevin, and that alone helped her communicate with him better than last time.

Kevin on the other hand was still keeping things from Brittany. Every morning when Kevin arrived at work, he received a little black gift box from an anonymous person with a note inside saying "I miss you." Kevin blocked Sybil from calling him after the first box, but the text messages still came in from anonymous numbers.

He was thrown off by how determined she was to be with him. He thought the sex was good, but not to the level to continuously pester him about it. Kevin figured as long as he kept ignoring her, she would get the picture and stop bothering him. Keeping Brittany out of this was the only thing that made sense to Kevin. The last thing he wanted was Brittany having doubts about him and Sybil dating again.

It wasn't until after a long day of showing homes to clients that Kevin decided to stop by The Sanctuary to see Brittany on a late Saturday evening. After about an hour, he decided to head home and finish some work at home. He came back out to his car, and found a note attached to his window.

He looked around the parking lot and snatched the note off of his polished Maserati. He opened the note and read "SHE DOESN'T DESERVE YOU." Frustrated and completely fed up he ripped the note up and unblocked Sybil to give her a call.

Sybil:

Hello?

Kevin:

Sybil I'ma say this in the most respectful way I can, but at this point you really starting to annoy me. Stay away from my place of business. Stay away from my girl's place of business and keep ya muhfuckin' hands off my car. Are we clear?

Sybil:

Kevin, I'm just showing you what you deserve. You need a real woman, like me.

Kevin:

I got a real woman and her name is Brittany

Sybil:

(giggles) You can't be serious.

Kevin:

Look Sybil, we hung out for a while it was cool but that was it. Brittany and I are back together, and we don't need you bothering our lives anymore.

Sybil:

You don't know what you want Kevin, one day you want me on the menu for dinner, the next you want Brittany. I don't mind sharing for a while, at least until you get it all out of your system.

Kevin:

Sybil stay the fuck away from us, or I'm put a restraining order on ya crazy ass.

Kevin hung up his phone, hopped in his car and sped off. Irritated from the level of boldness Sybil just threw at him had him completely aggravated.

He knew in order to protect his relationship from Sybil, he was going to have to tell Brittany what's been going on. He looked down at his phone and blocked her number from calling him again. Hoping that her infatuation with him was finally over. The last thing he wanted was Sybil coming around Brittany with brand new lies.

5. DREW

Sunday came around, and they decided to get out of the house and grab a bite to eat at Bar Taco. They sat at the bar to get a few drinks, while they waited for a table. Minutes after they sat down Brittany noticed Selena across the room having dinner with someone. She looked flawless. Her hair was freshly blown out with big loose brown curls bouncing with every laugh and smile.

Brittany:

Oh my gosh Kev look it's Selena, let's go say hi.

Kevin:

Oh, she must have had the evening off today.

Kevin and Brittany casually walked over to say hello. When Brittany got close enough, she noticed the man she was sitting with looked familiar. Once she reached the table it was too late, she stood there frozen, somehow finding the words to blurt out.

Brittany:

Hey Selena, so nice to see you!

Selena:

Brit, Kev! Heeyyyy! This is Drew the guy I was telling you about at your spa.

Brittany:

Oh right, nice to finally meet you Drew, this is my boyfriend Kevin.

Drew:

Nice to meet you man.

Kevin:

What's up man, nice to meet you.

Brittany:

We saw you sitting here from the bar we wanted to come over and say hi. Make sure you come by The Sanctuary soon, I miss your face.

Selena:

I will babe, you two have a good night.

Kevin:

See you at the office Selena.

Brittany grabbed Kevin by the hand and rushed back to the bar. She was in complete shock. Drew had been sending her roses for weeks, and he's been dating Selena the whole time.

Kevin:

You okay baby?

Brittany:

This cannot be happening.

Kevin:

What's wrong?

Brittany:

Drew was a regular at Ebony. He always wanted us to be something, but long story short, ever since he heard I was out of the club, he's been sending roses to The Sanctuary almost 3 times a week. Even the same day Selena came to the spa and said she was dating someone new. She told me and Melissa she was on her way to dinner with him.

Kevin:

Melissa? You still fuckin her?

Brittany:

KEVIN.

Kevin:

Alright... continue. Are you saying her new dude wants to be with you?

Brittany:

I'm sure he doesn't anymore after seeing you, but what about Selena? She looks so happy. Should I tell her?

Kevin:

If he reaches out to you then yes, but if he stops after this, then maybe things are getting serious between them and there's no reason to speak on it.

Brittany:

Drew has loved me for years.

Kevin:

Do you love him?

Brittany:

Of course not, baby. I'm just in shock that's all.

Kevin:

Why didn't you tell him we were seeing each other again?

Brittany:

Because baby, we hardly talk. Most of the time he's talking to himself when he texts me, because I hardly reply. I thought he'd catch the hint.

Kevin:

That's not how it works Brittany, you have to be honest with these niggas or they'll keep trying you. You know better.

Brittany:

Kev don't start, I just wanted to make sure you knew the truth.

Kevin:

Well thank you for telling me.

Host:

Kevin your table is ready for you.

As they walked over to the table Kevin received an anonymous text message. He looked at the message and froze at what he saw.

Brittany:

What's wrong baby? If you feel uncomfortable, we can leave.

Kevin:

No, no its not, it's Sybil. I didn't want you to get upset, but now I think this is getting out of hand.

Brittany:

What are you talking about?

Kevin:

Sybil has been harassing me almost every day with pictures and text messages from random numbers after I blocked her. It's starting to get weird.

Brittany:

What is she saying?

Kevin:

I'm embarrassed to say, but you can see for yourself.

Kevin handed his phone over to Brittany and she was completely taken back by the paragraphs, she was sending along with naked photos and details about their intimate moments together.

Kevin:

She left a note on my car saying, "she doesn't deserve you," while my car was parked in front of The Sanctuary; I was only there for about an hour. I'm starting to feel like she's stalking me.

Brittany:

Get the fuck out of here. She got me fucked up. I'm putting an end to this right now.

Kevin:

What are you going to do?

Brittany:

I'm calling her.

Sybil:

Hi baby I knew you would eventually call me back. I miss you.

Brittany:

This isn't Kevin, this is Brittany. I don't know what the fuck is wrong with you but it stops today. Kevin and I are back together, and we would like it if you left us both alone. I'm having you blocked and if you show up on mine or Kevin's property again, we'll have you arrested.

Sybil:

(LAUGHS) Kevin didn't tell you about us and you're clearly upset. It's okay sweetie just accept that you're old news. I'm the one putting him to bed at night, he enjoys every bit of it.

Brittany:

You're fucking crazy Sybil, there's plenty of fish in the sea get the fuck off mine.

Without even waiting for her response she hung up the phone and handed it back to Kevin. The waitress arrived with their drinks just in time. She grabbed her drink and looked up at Kevin.

Brittany:

Block those numbers, and if she shows up to your office I'm going to beat her ass, cheers.

Kevin:

I don't know if I'm turned on right now or concerned.

Brittany:

This is Atlanta Kev, you got to be aggressive, or these bitches will always come for what's rightfully yours. I learned that quick at Ebony.

Kevin:

I don't know Brit, a restraining order sounds like the best thing for my company. I can't have a liability like that on my name.

Brittany:

I agree 100% for both of our names.

Brittany stepping in brought Kevin so much relief telling her. She was on his side and they were communicating better. Their progress confirmed his decision to give their relationship a second chance. Kevin was grateful Brittany was on his side this time. The way she handled Sybil, made him realize that Brittany did consider him.

Finally, it was beginning to feel like Brittany and Kevin were on the same page. Now that Sybil was no longer in both of their lives; It was time to finally get back to building their lives together.

6. Unexpected Guests

Monday morning came and Brittany was back at The Sanctuary taking care of business. She was getting ready to take a lunch break when she heard a knock at the door. She looked up to find a man standing behind a huge bouquet of red roses. He poked his head around the roses so she could see his face.

Drew:

Good Morning beautiful.

Brittany:

DREW…

Drew:

Hey… I miss you, haven't seen you lately.

Brittany:

No, Andrew you don't miss me. What exactly are you doing? I'm back with Kevin, and you're with Selena now, or did you forget?

Drew:

You said that as if it means something. You know I always loved you Sapphire. I'm having fun with Selena but she's not you, you're special to me baby, we can move forward without them.

Brittany:

Drew we can't see each other anymore, I'm sorry, I love Kevin.

Drew:

You love Kevin? Ha-ha are you serious so you told him about our arrangement?

Brittany:

YES, I'm serious... whatever arrangement we had is over now.

Drew:

Yeah aight, how much you want to fall out of love with Kev, I know you, everything has a price.

Brittany:

Drew, I got my own money I'm good, you can't put a price on real love.

Drew:

Yeah okay, who ever got the bigger bag always wins. You just waiting on something bigger than me and Kev to jump off the cliff for. It's only a matter of time.

Brittany:

Fuck you Drew and take these weak ass flowers with you.

Drew:

No need to curse at me I'm just saying, I love you, I'll always be here for you, but I been fucking with you on and off for years Saph, I know how you move.

Brittany: You don't know shit.

Drew:

OKAY, I hope so.

Brittany:

Tell Selena I said hi.

Drew smirked and nodded his head before he walked out of Brittany's office. She made sure the coast was clear, then quickly grabbed her phone to call Melissa.

Brittany:

Come on answer, answer, answer the phone!

Melissa: Hello?

Brittany: Melissa!

Melissa:

Hey girl, how are you? I was just thinking about you, I had such a long night.

Brittany:

I need to talk to you asap! Can we meet somewhere?

Melissa:

Yeah meet me at Southern City Kitchen in 20, I'm starving.

Brittany: Okay perfect.

Brittany hung up and immediately dialed Blue. If anyone could help her deal with Drew, it would definitely be her. Blue was still dancing at Club Ebony and didn't have plans of leaving anytime soon. She knew Drew as a regular, before he caught a thing for Brittany, so she was really familiar with how he moved.

Blue:

What's up bitch, where you been?

Brittany:

Girl, I need you to meet me somewhere asap.

Blue:

You okay girl?

Brittany:

I'm fine there's just a lot going on, can you meet me at Southern City Kitchen? I'm meeting Melissa there in about 20.

Blue:

O-o-oh sexy ass Melissa coming, I'm on my way.

Brittany:

I can't stand you.

Blue:

I'll see you in 20 Brit.

Melissa walked in looking not like her usual self her hair was a mess, her false lashes were hanging off of her eye lids, and her eye makeup was slightly smeared. Brittany stood up in confusion and gave Melissa an uncomfortable hug.

Brittany:

Melissa have you slept at all?

Melissa:

Kind of, it's just been a long night, but what's going on? Is everything okay?

Brittany:

No, shit is getting complicated quick, and I don't know what to do.

Melissa:

What happened?

Just as Brittany tried to find the words of where to start, Blue walked in with her eyes directly on Melissa. She had a brand new white Chanel bag with some Chanel sneakers to match.

Blue:

Hey ladies.

Melissa:

Hey Blue. I haven't seen you in a while.

Blue:

I know Melissa, so nice to see you baby. Britt likes to keep you all to herself.

Brittany:

Okay y'all focus. Let me spill the tea.

Blue:

Please...

Melissa:

What happened?

Brittany:

'Member when Selena was heading out that day you came in?

Melissa:

How could I forget; she looked amazing.

Brittany:

She was on her way to meet a guy she has been dating. Last night me and Kev went to Bar Taco and seen her sitting down with this mystery man. As soon as Kevin and I get close enough, I realize it was Drew!

Blue:

Oh, hell nah.

Melissa:

Who is Drew?

Brittany:

And he had the nerve to come into my spa today with flowers saying we should leave them and be together.

Melissa:

He did what?

Blue:

How much he talkin?

Brittany:

Girl nothing worth leaving Kev for. Things are going well; I'm making my own money, and Drew is just Drew.

Blue:

Idk girl he hasn't been at Ebony like he used to, and when he is there, he's getting dances from a bunch of new bitches who resemble you.

Brittany:

Shut up Blue.

Blue:

I'm serious, he would have emptied his bank account for Saph, if she would have entertained his ass a little more. He loved her.

Brittany:

Money can't buy happiness.

Blue:

Girl do you know who you talking to? We both know money can buy your happiness.

Brittany:

Blue, things are different now. I changed for the better.

Blue:

Yeah, you can stop eating bacon but that doesn't mean it still doesn't smell good, you feel me?

Melissa:

Did you and Drew ever date?

Brittany:

Not really, he used to pay my bills from time to time, take me to dinner, and buy me a purse here and there. We had sex once after a drunk night and a couple days later Kenzo showed up.

Melissa:

Who is Kenzo?

Blue:

A nigga even I would throw it all away for, and he chose Saph.

Brittany:

Fine as hell and has a net worth of 1.3 billion dollars.

Blue:

He had the stupid bag. But he was smart. He didn't have to go crazy and spend it all in one night like most niggas do with temporary bread. He was selective and smooth. He would buy a private cabana, and send for a few women he already noticed on his way in. If he liked you, moments after he would leave, he would have his driver offer you an invitation to his penthouse. If you accepted, his driver would wait for you to get off and escort you to the top floor and into a room where possibly other women are waiting as well.

Once you turn in your phone and belongings you get paid to literally talk and chill all night in his sky-high dream home, and you always leave with gifts. One time I left with 4 Cartier bracelets for smoking with him. After he sent for Brittany, he only sent for Brittany every time he came back to Atlanta. Kenzo was giving Brittany so much money, we didn't know what to do with it. We went shopping every day.

Brittany:

And my dumb ass didn't save any of it. I thought I hit the jackpot.

Blue:

Brittany was only showing up to work once a week to show face when he came in town, but she was good once Kenzo came around. If Kenzo shows up in town, you go period. He's more than just a bill paid or a Chanel bag, he's an experience; he changes your life forever.

Melissa:

So, what happened between you TWO? Where is he?

Brittany:

(sigh) He travels a lot for work. He asked me to come with him, because he was going to be living out of the country for a year, but I was in school at the time. I wanted to chase my dream, but he didn't want me to do anything but be his woman. He gave me a choice to quit school and come with him or stay here and risk losing him to someone else.

I asked if we could compromise, let me finish school and I'll come after. Kenzo didn't like that answer. He left without saying a word and changed his number. I haven't heard from him since.

Blue:

I still can't believe you fucked that up. You could have been somewhere on the top floor of one of his penthouses right now, and you were thinkin' bout a SPA? She's stupid.

Brittany:

Bitch who you tellin'? I still regret it.

Blue:

Changed Brittany wouldn't regret it, would she?

Melissa:

I don't think you're stupid Brittany. Look where you are now, you own a spa; it worked out for the better.

Brittany:

Fuck Kenzo, that's the past, and he ain't comin' back. The real issue is Kevin, Andrew, and Selena. Should I tell Kevin or let it go?

Melissa:

What about Selena? Are you going to tell her?

Brittany:

Oh my Gosh.

Blue:

What.

Brittany:

Selena is calling me!

Melissa:

Right now?

Brittany:

Yes!

Melissa:

Answer. I guess just see what she wants. It may not be about Drew.

Brittany:

What if it is?

Blue:

Bitch answer the phone.

Brittany:

... Hey Selena, how are you?

Selena:

Hey Brit, I think you should come by the office as soon as you can.

Brittany:

To your office?

Selena:

Yes, well Kevin's office. I can't really explain, but I think Kevin's in trouble. It's Sybil, she showed up and he asked her to leave, and well I think it's best you come up here, and we can talk in person.

Brittany:

Where's Kevin?

Selena:

He's talking to the police.

Brittany:

The police!? Who the fuck called 12?

Blue:

(whispers) Oh hell nah.

Brittany:

I'm on my way Selena, thank you for letting me know.

Melissa:

What happened Brit?

Brittany:

I'll explain later, can y'all ride with me to Kevin's office?

Melissa:

Yes of course, I'll park my car at The Sanctuary since it's close by, and we can head over together.

    Brittany arrived at Kevin's real estate office and was immediately alarmed by the sight of cop cars and an ambulance driving off. Brittany slammed on her brakes, parked her brand new silver Mercedes, unfastened her safety belt and rushed inside. She approached his office door, only to find his neatly organized space had been hit by either a tornado or a crazy bitch. There were papers all over the ground, broken glass and ripped up photos of Kevin and Sybil together. Today had turned into a Monday afternoon nightmare.

Brittany walked in and looked at Kevin in complete confusion. A look of complete disappointment weighed on his spirit when he finally locked eyes with Brittany.

Brittany:

Kev, what is going on?

Kevin:

Baby she left pictures of us from Rich's wedding all over my desk. She showed up in lingerie under a jacket. I asked her to leave or I would call the cops, and she started yelling and banging her head against the wall! I tried to grab her and stop her, but she just started attacking me, trying to kiss me and yank at my clothes. Her head started bleeding all over the place, the bitch is crazy.

Selena:

I heard some noise so I came in and saw her attempting to hurt herself. It was absolutely disturbing. Listen we need to get these cops out of here. This is not a good look for our company at all Brittany. We have worked too damn hard getting the clientele we have, the last thing we need is any type of liability to jeopardize our business relationships. We have to do something about this now; help me get them out of here.

Drew:

Hey baby…

Selena:

Drew! Hey sorry I haven't had a chance to look at my phone. There was an incident with our CEO, I don't think right now is going to be a good time.

Drew:

It's okay, I thought I'd drop in and take you to lunch. I was just worried when I didn't hear back from you, it's not like you to go so long without responding.

Selena:

That's so sweet of you, but unfortunately, I don't think I'll have time for lunch now.

Drew:

Hey Brittany, how are you?

Brittany:

Fine! Look y'all we need to figure out how to get rid of Sybil, she's going to start fucking up our money and we can't have that.

Drew:

SYBIL?

Brittany:

You know her too?

Drew:

Sybil Cannon?

Brittany:

YES, Sybil Cannon

Drew:

Oh my God.

Brittany:

Drew if you know something speak up.

Drew:

She's my ex-wife.

Brittany:

… Andrew CANNON… how did I fucking miss this?

Selena:

How did you know his last name?

Brittany:

(heavy sigh) Wait let's stay on track real quick. She's been harassing Kevin for months, have you seen her act like this before?

Drew:

I guess you could say that.

Kevin:

Sybil just banged her head against the wall until she bled because I wouldn't fuck her in my office, if you know something please tell us, so we know how to handle her.

Drew:

Sybil is bipolar, she was diagnosed a year before we got married. It was controllable at first but she didn't like taking her meds, she started using other drugs to control her mood while she worked, but things just kept getting worse with us. I started going out more so I didn't have to be home. But she started stalking my every move. When Sybil found out I was seeing Saph at Ebony, she started tracking what I was buying her on our bank statements.

Selena:

Sapphire, as in Brittany? You two know each other?

Brittany:

Selena I just found out when we saw you at the restaurant the other day. I wanted to tell you but you looked happy, and I'm back with Kev now. I didn't get a chance; Everything was happening so fast, but I promise I was going to tell you.

Selena:

So, you knew you dated Brittany and never told me?

Drew:

Baby it wasn't like that.

Selena:

What the hell was it like then?

Kevin:

Look y'all, I get there's a lot of weird shit going on, but let's focus on the bigger picture. We got a crazy bipolar woman that might have it out for both me and

Brittany, if what Drew is saying is true. Think about it Brit; it makes perfect sense of why she was trying to pursue me so hard. She thought you ruined her marriage, so she went after our relationship.

Rich:

Damn bro who did you piss off? Man your office is trashed! Melissa? What are you doing here?

Kevin:

Selena I'm going home for the day. I'll have my assistant cancel my meetings and you're also welcome to reschedule anything you had for the day, so we can regroup. I think we should all go back to my place and figure out what the hell is going on with all of us.

Selena:

I agree Kevin I'll be there after I reschedule my 3:45.

Kevin:

Perfect I'll see you soon. Drew, I advise you to come so we can get all the info we need on Sybil. I need to understand exactly what we're dealing with.

Brittany:

Okay, baby let's get you cleaned up and get out of here.

Melissa:

I'll ride with Rich.

Blue:

I'm riding with Melissa!

Brittany:

Okay I'll see you soon girl.

7. Fool me once shame on you

Everyone hopped in their cars and drove to Kevin's place. Awkward was an understatement once everyone was in the same room together. Everyone was sitting down like they were trapped in after school detention.

Everyone's eyes glared back and forth at each other in complete confusion of what the hell was going on. Selena and Drew sat together with eyes on Brittany and Kevin, while Brittany and Kevin glared at Melissa and Rich sitting comfortably like they didn't just have a divorce, and Blue stood there with eyes on everyone soaking up everyone's drama before the tea got spilled.

Kevin:

Alright Drew since you know Sybil the best, we're going to need to know as much as possible. Has she tried hurting herself before?

Drew:

Twice. Which led to the divorce.

Brit:

How is this unstable woman capable of running multiple businesses?

Drew:

It's strange. When she focuses on her businesses, she's fine, but once she wants something or someone, she'll do anything to get it. She's an extremely dedicated woman that's for sure.

Kev:

How long has she been off medication?

Drew:

She never really liked taking them. I think she always was bipolar, but after her miscarriage, she was never the same; she spiraled. I tried to be a good husband, but I'm from the streets. I love women, I got needs. She wasn't the fun Sybil I fell in love with.

She was a dancer when we met, she was driven, and passionate. Everything changed for the better but once we got married, it triggered something inside her, and she became this control freak. She turned into this extremely codependent headache. She wanted to be the boss of every single thing. I started going out more to get out the house, and then I met Saph at the club.

She had dreams and vision just like Sybil, but she moved differently. Saph was softer, sweeter... I had to save her. Once she saw my bank statements, of how much I was spending on Sapphire, she started going to Ebony in disguise, and would sit at the bar while Saph would dance for me. I didn't figure this out until I came home one day and there were pictures of Sapphire giving me a lap dance all over the crib.

We argued until I finally admitted I didn't love her anymore. That's when she went crazy. She put a tracking device on my car, and started leaving notes wherever I was, telling me to be a good husband, or telling me she loves me. After 3 months of fighting, I couldn't take it anymore. I filed for divorce.

Once my restraining order went through, she disappeared. Last I heard she was back on track and her business was doing phenomenal in Miami. I had no idea she even came back to Atlanta.

Brittany:

She had it out for me from the very beginning. That's why she was so nice and making friends with me. She purposely wanted to hear about my relationship, so she could ruin what she thought I ruined for her. It all makes sense now.

Blue:

It takes one good ass whoopin' to teach a bitch a lesson she'll never forget.

Selena:

Blue, it's way bigger than an ass whoopin', we have businesses to run and clients to keep happy.

Blue:

I'm just saying, every time I had to drag a bitch, she never fucked up my paper again.

Brit:

As tempting as that sounds, Selena is right. We got to get rid of her the legal way.

Melissa:

I agree you don't need anything jeopardizing your place of business. Especially someone unstable.

Rich:

I think we should pull up on her at the hospital, and just let her know whatever game she's playing is over now.

Brittany:

What do you think Drew? If we sit her down and try to talk, do you think it would help?

Selena:

I think the two of you should go talk to her, since you two are the core of why we're all in this mess.

Brittany:

Selena, listen I'm sorry about all of this. I never wanted to be with Drew.

Drew:

Don't start something you can't finish Saph.

Brittany:

First of all, my name is Brittany, Andrew. And I am not afraid to address the truth, are you? 'Cause with everything happening right now we all got shit to lose.

Kevin:

What exactly is the truth? 'Cause somehow me and Selena are in the dark, you two seem to have more going on than you both are telling us.

Selena:

Was this planned too? Did you know me and Brittany knew each other?

Drew:

No, of course not baby.

Brittany:

Andrew loaned me a large amount of money to finish renovation fees for The Oasis room. After my new place and my new car, I didn't have all the money I needed up front. Our agreement was to meet every Tuesday night and in return he would pay off my credit card bill and fund my skin care product. I paid him in full a week ago to be done with our agreement. Drew showed up at my office with roses, after I saw Selena with him at Bar Taco.

Kevin:

So, you lied to me?

Brittany:

I didn't lie to you Kevin. I just didn't want to tell you everything. I just got your trust back, the last thing I wanted was for you to think that I was the same person that led to our breakup last time.

Kev:

Well that's exactly what I think. What the fuck you mean you meet with him every Tuesday night? You should have told me everything Brittany. How can we build trust, if you keep leaving me in the dark? We got a crazy bitch stalking us, and you don't think the truth would protect us right now?

Selena:

Look, we all were misled. I think we should take some time to cool off and get back on track. I'm going to call the hospital to check the status on Sybil. Once we talk to her maybe we can put all this behind us peacefully, in a mature manner.

Selena called the hospital only to find out that Sybil was checked in but disappeared hours later. Sybil was nowhere to be found, and both of her phones were going straight to voicemail. Kevin and Brittany's friends sat in the living room lost thinking about which route to take to find a solution.

Selena:

The hospital said if she turns up to let them know. She was checked in but never discharged, and now she's nowhere to be found.

Blue:

So, this crazy bitch escaped the hospital and y'all still don't want to beat her ass?

Rich:

I'm with Blue this time, Sybil is trippin'.

Selena:

The best option is for us to contact our lawyers and let them handle everything else moving forward. As for you Andrew. We no longer need your services you can let yourself out.

Drew:

Selena?

Selena:

Don't even try it. The sex wasn't even that good, and nobody wants to see you beg in public, have a nice day.

Drew:

Your loss sweetheart, y'all have a nice life.

Rich:

Stay Sybil free bro

Melissa:

Rich.

Rich:

I'm just sayin.

Melissa:

We're going to give you and Kevin some time alone, Brittany. Call us if you need anything. My father's a great lawyer, I'll give him a call, so he can give you guys the best legal advice to make sure you guys are kept safe.

Brittany:

Thanks Melissa, I'll see you soon.

Blue:

I'm going to catch a ride with them back to my car, I'll see you later Brit.

Brittany:

Call me later.

Rich:

Don't stress it bro, everything will go back to normal before you know it.

Kevin: It sure doesn't feel like it.

Brittany:

Listen Selena can we talk?

Selena:

It's okay Brittany, it wasn't your fault, you didn't know.

Brittany:

I love Kevin. I am not the same girl Drew fell for. He fell in love with someone who no longer exists.

Selena:

Trust me, I know. You're not the same woman I met when you walked into my office for your interview. You're a boss now, and if anyone sees how much your mind has grown it's me and Kevin. Get some rest, I'll see you next week, schedule me in for Friday.

Brittany:

That's a bet girl. Kevin I'm sorry, I should have put everything on the table when we got back together.

Kevin:

Yeah you should have, and I should have told you sooner about Sybil. Let's just try to put this behind us. Both of them are out of our lives for good. Now everything can get back to normal.

Brittany:

Speaking of normal, is it weird that Rich and Melissa are so comfortable with each other? It's almost like they're more comfortable with each other now than when they were an actual couple.

Kevin:

Every time I think I have them two figured out they surprise me. Hell, every time I think I have you figured out you surprise me.

Brittany:

Oh yeah? Well then, I should keep it going then right...

Kevin:

Right.

Brittany:

Come here. It's been a long ass day.

Brittany started undressing in front of Kevin. After a long day of chaos, it was time to unwind. She let her clothes drop to the ground as she wrapped her arms around

Kevin's neck. He picked her up and laid her across his island counter in the kitchen. Kevin stroked Brittany's nipples with his tongue while she released soft moans and heavy breaths.

He kissed all over her firm caramel skin until he reached the moist gift in between her legs. Soft moans turned into whispers of I love you as he sent her into pure ecstasy. They released all their troubles all over Kevin's house until they fell asleep.

8. Fool me twice, shame on me

Kevin and Brittany were able to get past the Sybil and Drew situation and finally move forward. Despite Brittany's unknown arrangement with Drew, Kevin decided that he couldn't hold Brittany accountable for anything that she decided to do while they weren't together. It disappointed him that she couldn't break things off sooner but knowing that she felt uncomfortable coming to him for money once before, it justified why she felt the need to handle it without him.

He loved Brittany enough to give their relationship a chance now that they removed all things necessary to fully commit to one another. It wasn't hard for him to forgive and forget, but he made it very clear if she had money issues again to always let him know first. She made him a promise and they never spoke about Drew again. Two months had gone by and nobody had heard a word about Sybil and Andrew Cannon.

Brittany had tried to call her phone a couple times, but it continuously went to voicemail. Kevin's lawyer assured him they would be fine and restraining orders would be placed for their protection against any future allegations Sybil might try to pull. Protecting the name of their self-made businesses, was far more important to them than some crazed woman seeking revenge for an ex-husband that Brittany had no desire to be with. After months of drama, everything was finally starting to go back to normal.

Another eventful day at The Sanctuary was taking place. Brittany was back at work trying out samples for her new skin care line called "Anointed." She invited Blue, Melissa, Selena, and Rich's girlfriend Joyce to have a spa day in the Oasis room and try out her new samples. The girls were enjoying their champagne and mingling when Natalie walked in to let Brittany know she had a guest arrive asking to speak to her.

Natalie:

Sorry to interrupt you Brittany, but you have a guest in the front asking to speak to you.

Brittany:

I'll be right there Natalie, thank you.

Brittany walked out of the Oasis room and walked over to her lobby area where she froze at the sight of an unexpected guest.

Kenzo:

It's nice to finally see you again Brittany.

Brittany:

Kenzo, what are you doing here?

Kenzo:

I came back for you, baby.

Brittany looked down and saw her phone ringing in her hand, it was Kevin. She stood there completely paralyzed. As she let her phone ring.

Natalie:

Brittany, is everything okay? Brittany, Kevin is calling on line 1. What would you like me to tell him... Brittany?

Thank you for reading "Pulsations of a Heartbeat: A second chance at love. Book 3" by PRINTHOUSE BOOKS; Author; T. Moniz. Please leave a review; we would love to know what you think.

www.PrintHouseBooks.com

VIP INK Publishing Group, Inc.

Atlanta, Georgia

www.ingramcontent.com/pod-product-compliance
Lightning Source LLC
Chambersburg PA
CBHW062109080426
42734CB00012B/2809